Featherstone

fantastic ideas for
teaching phonics

ALISTAIR BRYCE-CLEGG

Published 2013 by Featherstone Education
Bloomsbury Publishing plc
50 Bedford Square, London, WC1B 3DP
www.bloomsbury.com

ISBN 978-1-4081-9397-6

Text © Alistair Bryce-Clegg 2013
Design © Lynda Murray
Photographs © Shutterstock

Printed and bound in China by C&C Offset Printing Co. Ltd., Shenzen, Guangdong

This book is produced using paper that is made from wood grown in
managed, sustainable forests. It is natural, renewable and recyclable.
The logging and manufacturing processes conform to the environmental
regulations of the country of origin.

10 9 8 7 6 5 4 3 2

To see our full range of titles visit **www.bloomsbury.com**

Acknowledgements
We would like to thank the staff and children of the following settings for their time
and patience in helping put this book together, including the use of a number of
photographs:

London Early Years Foundation, Emli Bendixen
Noah's Ark Pre-School
Edmondsley Primary School
Thomas More Roman Catholic Primary School
Woodhouse Community Primary School
The Arches Primary School
Cosy Foundation (Cosy Direct)

Also thanks to Fee Bryce-Clegg.

Contents

Introduction

By the time that children are ready to begin to use phonic skills in their reading and writing, they are likely to have heard a range of words and phrases and used them in their own talk. The first step in the phonics journey is to help children to listen to the sounds in the environment around them and to discriminate between the different sounds. Children need lots of opportunities to listen to these sounds and to use their listening skills to try and identify and match them. The ability to listen carefully and discriminate between the individual sounds is crucial to their phonic progress. Once they have become familiar with this technique, children can use it to identify the different sounds that exist within words and then begin the sometimes tricky job of matching them to letter shapes. This in turn will enable them to make and read words.

Research shows that the most effective way of teaching young children to read is to teach phonics in a structured way, starting with the easiest sounds and progressing through to the most complex ones. Almost all children who receive good teaching of phonics will learn the skills they need to tackle new words in reading and writing. They can then go on to read any kind of text fluently and confidently, and to read for enjoyment.

It is true that if a child does not learn to read then they cannot read to learn. It is also true that maximum engagement will produce maximum attainment, especially where children in the Early Years are concerned. The English language can be complicated when it comes to reading it or writing it down. Different letters often make different sounds depending in whether they are at the beginning, middle or end of a word sometimes their sound changes depending which other letters they are next to or even if there is a letter like an 'e' next door but one!

This complexity can often make the teaching of phonics difficult (and a little dull!). The children that we work with need to be motivated and excited about their learning. Maximum engagement in the activities that we plan for them will give us the maximum potential for attainment. Linking what children need to learn about phonics to what they really enjoy is the key to long-term success. In this book Alistair has collected 50 ideas to help to inject some high level engagement into even the dullest phoneme string!

Food allergy alert

When using food stuffs to enhance your outdoor play opportunties always be **FOOD allergy !** mindful of potential food allergies. We have used this symbol on the relevant pages.

Skin allergy alert

Some detergents and soaps can cause skin reactions. **SKIN allergy !** Always be mindful of potential skin allergies when letting children mix anything with their hands and always provide lots of facilities to wash materials off after they have been in contact with the skin. Watch out for this symbol on the relevant pages.

Dressing-up bag

What you need:

- **Dressing-up bag/box**
- **Various items of clothing that begin with the initial sounds that you are teaching or reviewing**

What to do:

1. If you are doing this activity for the first time, name all of the items with the children as you put them into the dressing-up bag.
2. Focus on the initial sound and make sure everyone has had a chance to practise it.
3. Children can then take it in turns to put their hand into the dressing-up bag.
4. They pull out one item of clothing.
5. They can only put it on if they can tell you what sound it begins with.
6. If they are not sure then the item goes back into the bag.
7. Repeat so all the children have a turn.

Taking it forward

- Ask the children to tell you the end, middle or all sounds of the item depending on how challenging you want to make the game.
- Put more than one item in the box with the same sound and ask the children to pair items that start with the same sound.

What's in it for the children?

The children are having the opportunity to listen for, identify and repeat initial sounds.

Alphabet soup

What you need:

- Alphabet cards
- Large pan
- Wooden spoon or ladle

Taking it forward

- Use dry alphabet pasta instead of laminated cards. Then at the end of the activity you can boil it up and let the children really eat it!

What's in it for the children?

The children are having the opportunity to practise recognising and repeating initial letter sounds.

What to do:

1. Give out the alphabet cards to the children.

2. Let the children take turns in naming the sound on their card and then adding it to the pot, giving it a stir.

3. When all of the letters have been added to the 'soup' ask the children to take turns in 'serving' themselves a letter.

4. Ask the children to make the letter sound that they take from the pot.

Flipping phonics!

What you need:

- Brown paper
- Laminator and pouches
- Permanent marker
- Frying pan
- Fish slice or spatula

What to do:

1. Use the brown paper to cut out small pancake shapes.

2. On one side of each pancake write a word that contains a long or short vowel sound e.g. if 'a' is the sound being learned 'cat' or 'take'.

3. On the other side of the pancake write the corresponding sound, for example 'long a' or 'short a'. So on the back of 'cat' would be 'short a', and on the back of 'take' would be 'long a'. Laminate each pancake for durability.

4. Place the pancakes in the pan with the word facing upwards.

5. The player chooses a pancake and states whether there is a long or a short vowel sound being used in the word.

6. They flip their pancake to check.

7. If they are correct they keep their pancake. If not, it goes back in the pan.

8. Continue play around the group until everyone has had a go.

50 fantastic ideas for teaching phonics

long a

Taking it forward

- Create pancakes with words that use consonants, consonant diagraphs and consonant clusters.

What's in it for the children?

Long and short vowel sounds can be difficult for some children to recognise and hear. This game gives them a chance to build on their existing knowledge while having some fun.

cake

sat

Phonic fishing

What you need:

- **Fish template** (A4 size)
- **Card**
- **Scissors**
- **Felt tip pens**
- **Suitable music**

What to do:

1. Cut out the same number of card fish as there are children playing the game.

2. Write an initial sound, diagraph or cluster onto each fish.

3. Ask the children to stand in a circle.

4. Put one fish at each child's feet with the sound facing up.

5. Play the music while the children walk around the fish in their circle.

6. When the music stops the children stop.

7. The adult asks 'Which little fish says ...(give one of the sounds)'.

8. The child who is in front of the corresponding fish identifies the sound and then steps inside the circle: they are caught!

9. Continue with the game until all the fish have been caught.

Taking it forward

- Ask the children who have been 'caught' to name a word that starts or contains their sound before they step into the circle.

What's in it for the children?

The children are having the opportunity to identify and practise initial sounds, diagraphs and clusters.

Bottle top blend

What you need:

- A number of plastic bottle tops
- Two bags or boxes
- Permanent marker
- Cardboard

Taking it forward

- Replace the vowels with more complex vowel diagraphs.

What's in it for the children?

The children are having the opportunity to use their skills of phonic recognition as well as blending those sounds together to create words.

What to do:

1. Write a letter of the alphabet on the top of each of the bottle tops.

2. Create more than one set of consonants and several sets of vowels.

3. Make two cardboard labels one for 'vowels' and one for 'consonants'.

4. Place all of the vowel bottle tops in a bag or box in front of the 'vowel' label and the consonants in a bag or box in front of the 'consonant' label.

5. The children take it in turns to take one vowel and two consonants from the pile.

6. If they can make a word, they score a point. If not their bottle tops go back into the bag or box.

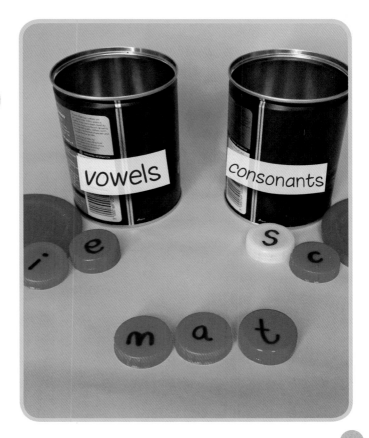

Football phonics

What you need:

- Goal post or goal mouth chalked onto a wall
- Sticky tack or strong tape
- Lightweight football
- Sticky backed Velcro
- Several 6 cm circles of card, laminated
- Whiteboard marker

What to do:

1. Write regular word endings such as at, ess, ob, ate, oam, op, ull etc. on some of the laminated circles of card.

2. Stick these around the goal mouth using the sticky tack or tape.

3. Stick one laminated circle on the football, using the Velcro.

4. On other laminated circles write a consonant diagraph or cluster e.g. ch, sh, th, wh, pr, spr, pl, cl etc. and affix these to the ball one at a time.

5. The children take it in turns to 'shoot' the ball into the goal.

6. Before they can kick it they have to make a word by marrying the card on the ball with one card around the goal.

7. The sound on the ball can be changed after each goal is scored.

ob

ess

p

ull

ate

ch

Taking it forward

- Make the sounds on the ball and around the goal more complex.

- Increase the number of options to make it easier.

- Decrease the number of options to make it harder.

What's in it for the children?

You will be using a game that is very popular with a large number of children to help them to use their phonic knowledge more effectively.

Recycled cereal search

What you need:

- **Lots of empty cereal boxes** (other boxes with writing on can be used)
- **Timer**
- **Alphabet cards**

What to do:

1. Put the cereal boxes into a pile in the middle of the table.
2. Shuffle the alphabet cards.
3. Take a card and show it to the children.
4. Start the timer.
5. The children have to find as many examples of the sound you have shown them in the text on the cereal boxes before the timer runs out.

Taking it forward

- Make the time shorter.
- Ask the children to find end and middle sounds of words.
- Ask the children to find words.

What's in it for the children?

The children are being given the opportunity to look for sounds, letters and words in a familiar context.

What's the sound Mr Wolf?

What you need:

- **Word cards**
- **Large space** (indoors or out)

What to do:

1. The adult is Mr or Mrs Wolf and they must stand some distance from the children.
2. The children call out *'What's the sound Mr Wolf?'*.
3. Mr Wolf then says or shows the children a word.
4. The children then sound out that word taking one step with each sound.
5. They stop and repeat the game with another word.
6. The first child to reach Mr Wolf is the winner.

Taking it forward

- Change the sounds for syllables.
- Make the words more complex.

What's in it for the children?

Children are using their phonic knowledge to distinguish the number of sounds in a word and not just the number of letters.

Find a friend

What you need:

- A selection of objects in a bag or box
- Other objects around your environment that start with the same initial sound as the objects in your bag or box
- Timer

Taking it forward

- Make the game more challenging by using end or middle sounds.
- Use rhyme or alliteration for a different challenge.

What's in it for the children?

The children will be having the opportunity to listen to, match and remember initial sounds. They will also have the opportunity to match sounds to objects.

What to do:

1. Children take it in turns to put their hand into the bag or box and pull out an object.
2. They must identify the initial sound of that object.
3. Once the initial sound has been identified the timer is started.
4. The children then have the length of the timer to find another object in your environment that starts with the same sound.
5. Once they have found something, they must leave their object next to it and return to their place.

May, widdle, flibble

What you need:

- A copy of the nursery rhyme 'Hey Diddle Diddle'

What to do:

1. Read the beginning of the nursery rhyme to the children.

2. Tell them that they are going to change the first three words of the rhyme.

3. The words can be real or nonsense as long as they follow the 'pattern' of the original e.g. May, middle, fiddle.

4. Generate a few examples with the children.

5. Then let them have a go.

Taking it forward

Apply this to any familiar nursery rhyme or song that they know such as 'Hickory, Dickory Dock', or 'Baa, Baa Black Sheep'.

What's in it for the children?

This activity usually generates a fair amount of hilarity! It gives you an opportunity to explore lots of aspects of phonics including alliteration, rhyme and how sounds make words similar and different.

50 fantastic ideas for teaching phonics

My pirate name is...

What you need:

- Alphabet cards
- Treasure chest
- Pirate props (optional)

What to do:

1. Have lots of discussion with the children first about pirate names and the sorts of words that are associated with pirates like 'Black Beard' and 'Pretty Polly'.

2. Put the alphabet cards into the treasure chest.

3. The children put their hand into the treasure chest and pull out a letter sound.

4. They have to invent a pirate name that starts with that sound.

5. The children can say 'I am ... the pirate'.

Ff

Fish

Zz

Zip

Taking it forward

■ Encourage the use of alliteration in the children's choices.

What's in it for the children?

The children are having the opportunity to apply their knowledge of something that they find fun and exciting to phonics.

Rhythm of a rhyme

What you need:

- Props that feature in familiar rhymes such as a spider for 'Incy Wincy', a star for 'Twinkle, Twinkle Little Star'

What to do:

1. Make a circle with the children.
2. Put the props into the middle of the circle.
3. If you are doing this for the first time, talk to the children about which nursery rhyme each prop represents.
4. Tell the children that you are going to clap the rhythm of one of the rhymes without any words.
5. The children have to listen carefully and identify which rhyme they think you are clapping.
6. Repeat your clapping if necessary.
7. The children must select the appropriate prop when they have identified the rhyme.

Taking it forward

- Reduce the number of props to make it easier.
- Increase the number of props for more challenge.

What's in it for the children?

This activity encourages the children to really listen to the rhythm of words and introduces them to how syllables form patterns within words.

Cobbler, cobbler

What you need:

- A copy of the rhyme 'Cobbler, Cobbler, Mend My Shoe'
- Selection of shoes, slippers, flip-flops etc

What to do:

1. Make a circle with the children.
2. Put the selection of shoes into the middle of the circle or table.
3. Identify each one and name it before the game begins.
4. The children begin by saying altogether, *'Cobbler, cobbler, mend me a shoe. Get it done by half past two'*.
5. The children then take it in turns to pick up a shoe and describe it using alliteration for example, *'Mine is a super, silky, soft slipper'*.

Taking it forward

- Ask the children to make up a rhyming sentence.
- Turn it into a memory game by asking each child to repeat what the child before them said.

What's in it for the children?

The children are having the opportunity to listen to and create alliterative phrases.

What's in my egg?

What you need:

- A number of hollow plastic eggs
- Small everyday objects like lentils, jingle bells, sand

Taking it forward

- Using larger objects and replacing the eggs with a box or container.

What's in it for the children?

In this activity you are encouraging the children to use their listening skills to identify sounds that they can hear.

What to do:

1. Put a different object or objects into each egg.
2. Keep an example of the object/s that you have used to show the children.
3. Seal the eggs.
4. Let the children shake the egg and listen carefully to the sound it makes.
5. Ask the children to match the sound inside the egg to the objects outside.

Backpack! Backpack!

What you need:

- A back pack
- Explorer's equipment and items that can be used for blending and segmenting e.g. m-a-p, h-a-t, s-t-r-ing, c-u-p, t-or-ch
- List of the equipment in the bag

What to do:

1. An adult says to the children, *'In my back pack you will find a …'*.
2. The adult then sounds out one of the items in the bag. For example, *'some s-t-r-ing'*.
3. The adult then asks *'What's in my back pack?'*.
4. The adult picks a child who thinks they know the answer. If they are right then they look in the back pack to see if they can find the item.

Taking it forward

- Using more complex spelling patterns for blending and segmenting.

What's in it for the children?

The children are listening to the sounds in words and then using their skills of blending and segmenting.

I was walking down the street

What you need:

- You could play this game following a walk around your local area or just based on the children's existing knowledge

Taking it forward

- Make the sounds more complex by using blends.

What's in it for the children?

The children have to listen to the sounds, blend them and then repeat with a small gap in between. This also helps to challenge and develop their memory skills.

What to do:

1. The adult starts by saying '*I walked down the street and I saw a/heard a….*'.

2. The adult then sounds out what they saw or heard e.g. c-a-r.

3. The children do not say the word, instead they make an appropriate sound to go with it e.g. brummmmmmm.

4. The adult then asks '*What was it?*'.

5. The children respond with the name of the object, animal or person.

The belly buster

What you need:

- **Circles of white paper** (the size of a dinner plate)
- **Coloured crayons**
- **Pencils**
- **Timer** (optional)
- **Letter cards**

Taking it forward

- Changing the criteria for the toppings: Only words that rhyme with…, only words with a short 'a' sound etc.

What's in it for the children?

The children are using their knowledge of letter sounds to be creative in making their pizzas. They are hearing, recognising and interpreting initial sounds in familiar words.

What to do:

1. The children work in groups.
2. Give each group a pre-cut circle and tell them it is their pizza base.
3. Explain that they are going to see which group can make the biggest 'belly buster' pizza.
4. They can only put toppings on their pizza that start with the letter sound you give them for example 'c': coffee, crisps, crackers, cucumber etc.
5. The children can draw or write the ideas that they come up with.
6. Once the timer has run out they must all stop and see who has the 'belly buster'.

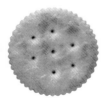

Postman

What you need:

- An envelope with a picture or word that starts with the same sound as the name of every child who will be playing the game
- A postman's bag and hat

What to do:

1. Put all of the envelopes into the postman's bag.
2. The children sit in a circle.
3. One child wears the postman's hat and has the bag.
4. The other children all chant 'Postman, postman one, two, three have you got a letter for me?'.
5. The postman takes an envelope out of his bag.
6. Either the postman identifies the initial sound of the picture on the envelope and then delivers it to the right person.
7. Or, the postman shows it to the group and the correct person identifies themselves.
8. If there is more than one person whose name starts with the sound on the postman's envelope, then the postman decides who to deliver it to.

Taking it forward

- To avoid boredom, change the postman after every few letters have been delivered.
- Rather than pictures, use words for the postman to read.

What's in it for the children?

The children are having the opportunity to hear, recognise and interpret initial sounds.

Sound twister

What you need:

- **The game Twister** (or make your own version)
- Laminator
- Velcro
- Circles of paper smaller than the circles on the Twister mat

Taking it forward

- Make the game harder by changing the complexity of the sounds that you use.

What's in it for the children?

The children are having the opportunity to learn and consolidate their phonic knowledge in a fun way.

What to do:

1. Write the sounds that you want the children to use on the paper circles and laminate them.

2. Stick one sound to each of the circles on the Twister game mat using the Velcro.

3. The sounds on the mat should match, so you place one sound on all of the green circles, a different sound on all of the red circles and so on.

4. Add the sounds on the circles to the spinner board.

5. The sound and the colour on the spinner board should now match the game mat.

6. One player spins and says the sound out loud.

7. The children on the mat must repeat the sound and then put their appropriate body part on the correct part of the mat.

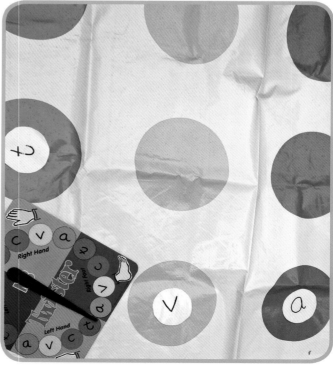

Give me a ...

What you need:

- A list of familiar words that the children will be able to blend and segment
- Pom-poms or shakers (optional)
- This is a great outdoor game!

What to do:

1. Split the children into two groups.
2. Tell them that they are going to be cheerleaders. Let them practise with their pom-poms and shakers.
3. An adult acts as the caller for their team.
4. The teams take it in turns to call out the individual sounds of a word, followed by the word itself.
5. The team that gets the most right and shouts the loudest is the winner.

Taking it forward

- Make the words and their spellings more complex.

What's in it for the children?

The children will be listening to sounds, remembering them, repeating them and using them to create words.

I'm shy!

What you need:

- Selection of musical instruments
- A curtain or screen

What to do:

1. Tell the children that you would like to play some music for them but you are shy.

2. Tell them that you are happy to play if you can do it from behind the curtain or screen.

3. Show them each of the instruments in your box, name them and then play them so that they are familiar with the sound.

4. Now play each of the instruments in turn from behind the curtain or screen and ask the children to identify which one you have played.

Taking it forward

- Play a particular rhythm on each instrument and get the children to clap the rhythm back before identifying the instrument.

What's in it for the children?

The children are using their listening skills to pick out individual sounds and matching them to an instrument using their memory.

When I'm calling you...

What you need:

- A selection of percussion instruments

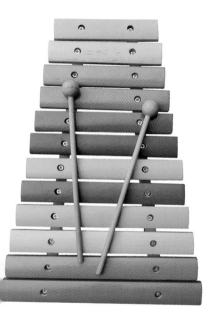

What to do:

1. Give each child a percussion instrument.

2. Either sit in a circle or position the children around the room with their instrument.

3. Call out a child's name and then say *'When I'm calling you'* (this is best done in the style of the 1936 hit for Jeanette Wilson and Nelson Eddy called 'Indian Love Call').

4. Now play out a rhythm on your instrument.

5. The child answers *'I will answer too'* (again in the style of 'Indian Love Call') and repeats the rhythm.

6. Repeat the process with a different child and another rhythm.

Taking it forward

- Make the rhythm more complex for more challenge.

- The use of 'Indian Love Call' is not essential to the game but it really makes the children (and adults) laugh!

What's in it for the children?

The children are rehearsing and consolidating their ability to listen, remember and repeat.

Look, a lion!

What you need:

- **A pair of binoculars**

What to do:

1. Take the binoculars and look through them.

2. Declare what you can see. The selected item must start with the same sound as the first word of your sentence. For example, *'Look, I see a lion!'*, *'Blimey! I see a banana'*, *'Fantastic, I see a fish!'*.

3. The children then join in adding words that start with the same sound.

4. They carry on until they run out of sounds or you 'see' something else.

Taking it forward

- Let the children lead with the binoculars.

- Sound out the words instead of saying them.

What's in it for the children?

The children are having the opportunity to listen to and recognise sounds in words and apply that knowledge to other words they know.

Granny's in the garden

What you need:

- **Alphabet cards**

What to do:

1. Shuffle the alphabet cards and then pick one.

2. Whatever letter is chosen must be the first sound of all of the 'key' words that the children use in a sentence.

3. The sentence always starts with a person, then a place, then a food then an animal. So for example, 'Granny is in the garden eating grapes with a gorilla' or 'Kathy is in the kitchen eating kiwis with a koala'.

4. The children take it in turn to think of a word that fits each stage of the story.

Taking it forward

- Remove some of the more difficult letters like 'x'.

- Give the children a set amount of time to come up with their answer.

What's in it for the children?

The children are exploring initial sound recognition as well as alliteration.

Three cows in a field

What you need:

- Pretend cows for props
- You can replace both the animal and the number to suit the children

Taking it forward

- Increase the complexity of the sounds.

What's in it for the children?

The children will be experiencing alliteration and building their vocabulary of words that start with the same sound.

What to do:

1. The adult begins a story and the children fill in the gaps.

2. The adult gives the children a subject and a sound.

3. The children then generate a word that is appropriate and begins with the correct sound.

4. For example: 'There were three cows in a field and their names began with 's'. They were called ... They all liked to eat food that started with ..., their favourites were ... They all wore coloured hats that started with 'b', they were ...'

5. The adult may want to think of some starting prompts before the game begins!

Shopping List

What you need:

- Small bags
- Any item you could buy from a shop

What to do:

1. Put the children into pairs in advance.

2. Create a bag of shopping that contains items that start with the same initial sounds as the names of the two players.

3. The children take it in turns to take items out of the bag.

4. They can keep the shopping if it starts with the same sound as their name, if not, they need to put it back.

Taking it forward

- Adding some items that do not start with the same sound as either child.

- Play it as a group activity with more items and more children.

What's in it for the children?

The children are able to practise discriminating, recognising and matching initial sounds.

Same as me

What you need:

- **Lots of objects** (or just use your whole environment, indoors and out)
- **Timer** (optional)

What to do:

1. Start by getting the children to clap the number of syllables in their name (this might take a little practice).

2. Once the children can do this, send them off on a mission to find other people and objects with the environment who have the same number of 'claps' as them.

aking it forward

Give the children less time for more of a challenge.

Ask the children to find objects with the same initial sound and the same number of syllables.

Vhat's in it for the children?

he children are listening and ecognising the pattern and rhythm ithin sounds and words.

odd one out

What you need:

- Quiet space
- **Visual props** (optional)

What to do:

1. Explain to the children that you are going to play an odd one out game.

2. If this is an unfamiliar concept then introduce the game by showing them three objects where one is the odd one out such as apple, grape and book.

3. Once the children have got the idea of the game then substitute the objects with spoken words.

4. The words can have the same first sound, they could rhyme or they could have the same number of syllables. Only ever use one criteria in any one game however, for example big, ball, snake or red, bed, helicopter.

Taking it forward

- Make the similarity between the words more complex.

What's in it for the children?

The children will have the opportunity to appreciate that some words can sound the same and some words start with the same letter sound.

On my holidays I went to...

What you need:

- Postcards or pictures as prompts

What to do:

1. In this game the children are going to rhyme words that they know with countries from around the world.

2. The adult begins by saying 'On my holidays I went to …' and then names a country.

3. The adult then carries on 'and I saw…'.

4. The children then suggest words that rhyme with the country. For example, 'On my holidays I went to Greece and I saw … some geese, the police, my niece…' and so on.

Taking it forward

- Put the children into groups or teams and awarding them points for every rhyming word they can come up with.

What's in it for the children?

The children are using their knowledge of words and sounds to select and then match rhyming words.

Old Macdonald had a...

What you need:

- Selection of farm objects
- Bag or box

Taking it forward

- Use objects other than animals to extend the game.

What's in it for the children?

The children have to use their listening skills and also be able to discriminate between the sounds that they hear in this game. They will be using their prior knowledge to match the sounds to a familiar animal or object.

What to do:

1. Put the selection of farm animals in the bag or box.
2. Chose one child to take an animal out of the box. They must not show it to the other children.
3. Instead of naming the animal the child should make the noise that the animal would make.
4. Invite the other children to say what the animal is.
5. Chose another child to select an animal and play again.

moo!

baa!

brmm!

A box full of...

What you need:

- **One matchbox per child** (or other small box or bag)
- **A range of small objects both indoors and out**
- **Marker pen**

What to do:

1. Give each child a matchbox.
2. On the top of their matchbox write a letter sound.
3. The children must go around your setting and try and fill their matchbox with items that begin with their given letter.
4. The child that gets the most is the winner.

Taking it forward

- Send this activity home as a weekend or holiday project.

What's in it for the children?

The children are applying their knowledge of initial sounds to everyday objects.

✚ Health & Safety

Small objects could pose a choking hazard. If you are at all concerned then use larger objects and a larger box.

What's my job?

What you need:

- Pictures or photos of people/faces

Taking it forward

- Make the jobs rhyme with the name.

What's in it for the children?

The children are recognising alliteration and having the opportunity to practise alliterative phrases.

What to do:

1. Tell the children that you are going to introduce them to a special group of people whose jobs all start with the same sound as their names.

2. Use the photographs as a prop and tell the children the name of the person in the photo. They have got to guess their job. For example, 'This is Pat and she is a pie maker', 'This is Dan and he is a dog trainer'.

Sandwich fillings

What you need:

- Sandwich making ingredients and equipment as a stimulus

What to do:

1. Show the children the sandwich ingredients and equipment and talk about choosing different fillings for sandwiches.

2. Tell the children that together you are going to make some imaginary sandwiches.

3. The first child starts by saying 'In my sandwich I like ...' and then suggests an ingredient.

4. The next child has to repeat what the first child has said and then add another ingredient that starts with the same sound.

5. Keep going until the list gets too long or you run out of ideas.

Taking it forward

- Make the list a rhyming list.
- Make the ingredients have the same number of syllables rather than start with the same sound.

What's in it for the children?

The children are listening to and recalling alliteration as well as having the opportunity to practice their knowledge of initial sounds.

Double trouble

What you need:

- **Number of objects in a box or bag** (make sure that there are groups of them that start with the same sound)
- **Clue cards where each of the objects has been segmented into its audible sounds** (c-ow, t-r-ai-n)

"

d-

d-o

d-o-g"

Taking it forward

- Make the possible number of correct objects greater.

What's in it for the children?

The children are having an opportunity to listen to and practise their oral blending and segmenting.

What to do:

1. The adult takes the first card and tells the child the are looking for something that starts with …. (if the adult has picked a card with d-o-g on it they will tell the child they are looking for objects that start with 'd').

2. The child selects all of the things that they can find that start with that sound.

3. The adult then gives the next sound clue (for d-o-g the adult would tell the child they were now looking for d-o)

4. The child selects all of the objects that match the sounds given.

5. The adult repeats the process until all of the sounds have been read out.

6. The child then repeats the sounds and blends them together to see if they are right.

t-r-ai-n
"

A robot came to tea

What you need:

- **Robot mask or cardboard box for a robot head**
- **Teaset**
- **Cutlery**
- **Food** (optional)

Taking it forward

- Create cue cards for the children to read with instructions for the robot on them.

What's in it for the children?

The children are having the opportunity to show their recognition of the sounds within words and how they can be blended and segmented.

What to do:

1. Set out the teaset and cutlery for tea.

2. Tell the children that you have invited a robot to tea but he only understands them if they speak like a robot.

3. One child puts on the robot mask or head and pretends to be the robot. He or she must ask for things in a robotic voice, for example, 'C-a-n I h-a-ve a d-r-i-n-k?'

4. The other children must offer the robot things and give instructions in the same robotic voice, 'S-i-t, d-ow-n'.

5. Continue with the game until all children have had a chance to show their knowledge of the sounds in words.

What you need:

- Paper or card to make 'Wanted' posters
- Pens and crayons

What to do:

1. Tell the children that you are going to create some 'Wanted' posters for master criminals who are on the loose.

2. Before the children can make the posters they will need a description of the criminal.

3. Work together to generate a description of a character.

4. All of the characteristics, likes and dislikes of the character you are describing have to start with the same sound. For example, *'This is Barry the bad bank manager, he steals bread and bath taps. He lives on a boat with a badger who eats bananas'*.

5. Once you have a few 'profiles' the children can draw or paint their 'Wanted' posters.

Taking it forward

- Make the criteria rhyme instead of having the same initial sound.
- Use blends at the beginning of words.

What's in it for the children?

The children are experiencing the use of alliteration as well as having the opportunity to use their phonic knowledge to find words that start with the same sound.

Crocodile in the river

What you need:

- A4 phoneme cards
- Large piece of blue fabric

What to do:

1. Lay the fabric on the floor like a river (if you are playing the game outside then you can use chalk instead).
2. Tell the children they have to cross the river, but a crocodile lives in it.
3. Assume the role of the crocodile and stand in the river.
4. The only way for the children to cross safely is for them to make a bridge.
5. They must make a bridge by laying three phoneme cards across the fabric to form a three letter word as a bridge.
6. The cards must spell a CVC word.

C

a

r

Taking it forward

- Make the river wider and the words longer.

What's in it for the children?

The children are given the opportunity to apply their phonic knowledge to recognition of sounds, blending and segmenting.

Rhyming hunt

What you need:

- Laminated cards with clues
- Treasure!

Top tip ★

This activity is great indoors or out.

What to do:

1. Create your rhyming hunt by giving clues that rhyme.
2. Each clue card will lead the children to the site of the next clue until you find the 'treasure'.
3. Use clues like 'Look under the big brown thing that rhymes with knee' etc.
4. Set up the hunt using the space inside and outside at your setting.
5. Give the children the first clue and set them on their way.
6. Remember to put some treasure at the end of the hunt!

Taking it forward

- Make the clues more complex and the rhymes more challenging.

What's in it for the children?

The children are having the opportunity to listen to the sounds of words, identify a rhyme and apply their prior knowledge to solve the clue.

t's mine

What you need:

- A bag or box
- Pictures or objects that begin with the same sound as the names of the children you are working with

What to do:

1. Fill the bag or box with objects.

2. The children take it in turns to say their first name and then look into the box or bag for an object that starts with the same sound.

3. When they have found something, they hold it up and say 'My name is Ben and this is my bear'.

4. The other children say if they are right or wrong.

5. If they are right they can keep the object. If not, it goes back in the box or bag and they try again.

aking it forward

Try using rhyming words rather than initial sounds.

What's in it for the children?

he children are using their listening kills to hear sounds that are the ame. They are also experiencing lliteration and recognition of initial ounds.

Sound meatballs

What you need:

- Yellow wool
- Bowl
- Tongs
- Brown paper
- Paper plates
- Marker
- Laminator and pouches

What to do:

1. Cut out the brown paper to look like meatballs.
2. Write an initial sound on each 'meatball' and laminate them.
3. Cut up the wool to look like spaghetti.
4. Mix the spaghetti and the meatballs together in the bowl.
5. Give each child a paper plate.
6. They must take it in turns to use their tongs to fish out the meatballs.
7. If they can identify the sound they can put the meatball on their plate.
8. See who can earn the most meatballs.

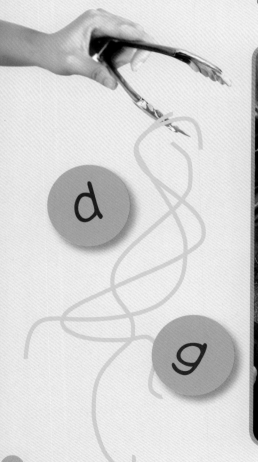

f

b

c

Taking it forward

- Write CVC words on the meatballs.
- Write rhyming words on the meatballs.

What's in it for the children?

The children are using their phonic knowledge to recognise and name initial sounds.

Wild west wet phonics

What you need:

- Tin cans
- Initial sound labels (laminated)
- Velcro
- Water pistol

What to do:

1. Attach the phonic labels to your cans using Velcro (this way the labels can be easily changed).
2. Line the cans up along a flat surface.
3. An adult calls out an initial sound.
4. A child shoots the corresponding can with his water pistol.

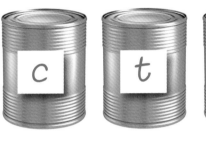

Taking it forward

- Use the same idea for rhyming words.

What's in it for the children?

The children have the opportunity to consolidate their knowledge of initial sounds while having some fun!

Code breaker

What you need:

- **Letter sound cards with a corresponding number on them** (a=1, b=2 etc)

- **Common simple words written in code for the children to solve** (c-a-t would be 3-1-20)

What to do:

1. Give the children some 'codes' to break. Hand out the letter cards and then write a code down for them to solve. They must find the corresponding letter for each number and arrange them in order to find the word.

2. When they have identified the letter sounds ask them to blend them together to make a word.

$$c = 3$$

$$n = 14$$

$$t = 20$$

Top tip ★

Children who are not confident with number recognition will need to work with an adult for this game.

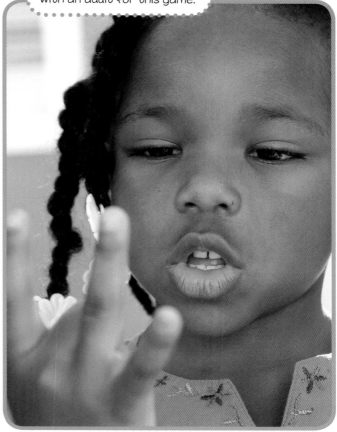

Taking it forward

Making the 'clue' words longer and more complex.

What's in it for the children?

The children are not only using their knowledge of initial sounds and having the opportunity to experience blending, they are also getting a bit of numeracy practice into the bargain!

Basket ball bin

What you need:

- Two footballs
- One bin

What to do:

1. Split the children into two teams.
2. The first player from each team takes the ball.
3. Call out an initial sound.
4. The first child who is able to say a word that starts with that sound gets a chance to score a 'basket' by throwing their ball into the bin.
5. The winners are the team who score the most points.

Taking it forward

- Get the children to blend more complex words.

What's in it for the children?

The children are having an opportunity to hear, recognise and then apply their knowledge of initial sounds.

etters and words

What you need:

- A whiteboard
- **Whiteboard markers** (one colour for each team)

aking it forward

Ask the teams to come up with more than one word for each sound.

Use rhyming words instead of phonemes.

Vhat's in it for the children?

he children are listening and lentifying initial sounds then pplying what they hear to their rior knowledge.

What to do:

1. Split your children into two teams.

2. Draw a classic 'noughts and crosses' grid with nine spaces.

3. Use a different colour marker for each team. A child from the first team shouts out a letter sound and tells you where to put it on the grid.

4. To gain the point another child from the same team must be able to name a word that starts with that sound.

5. The first team to get three in a row wins.

Roll the ball

What you need:

- Large soft ball
- Picture cards of CVC words

Taking it forward

- Roll the ball to create a rhyming string.

What's in it for the children?

The children are using their knowledge of phonics and also their ability to blend sound to create words.

What to do:

1. Children sit in a circle.
2. Show the group a picture card.
3. The child with the ball says the first letter sound of the CVC word.
4. They then role the ball to another child in the circle who says the next letter sound and so on.
5. Continue with other cards.

Zip

a bottle of sounds

What you need:

- Large drinks bottle
- Scissors
- Phonic labels
- Lots of objects that start with the same initial sound

What to do:

1. With scissors, CAREFULLY cut around a third of your bottle along the top of the label.

2. Remove the label.

3. Collect a number of items that begin with the same initial sound.

4. Put the items into the bottle by squeezing the bottle at either end of your cut and 'posting' them in.

5. Cover your incision with a label.

6. Encourage the children to turn the bottle and name the objects they can see.

Taking it forward

Create a number of bottles for each initial sound that the children learn.

Create other bottles for blends and diagraphs.

What's in it for the children?

The children are having the opportunity to look for, identify and repeat initial sounds.

Magnets in the snow

What you need:

- **Magnetic letters**
- **Fake snow** (or polystyrene packing)
- **Water**
- **Large container**
- **Magnet**

What to do:

1. Make up the fake snow according to the instructions on the packet using the water.

2. Hide the magnetic letters in the 'snow'.

3. Get the children to use a magnet to try and 'catch' a magnetic letter.

4. If the children can name the letter sound, they can keep it.

5. If not it goes back in the snow.

Taking it forward

- Ask the children to use the letters that they have found to make a word.

What's in it for the children?

The children are using their skills of recognition and phonic knowledge to identify and name initial sounds.

Wordy washing line

What you need:

- A washing line
- Small clothes (socks work well)
- Wooden pegs
- Permanent marker
- Timer

Taking it forward

Ask the children to create more complex and challenging words.

What's in it for the children?

Here children are using their phonic knowledge to enable them blend sounds into words.

What to do:

1. Put a selection of key sounds that the children are learning onto the pegs with the permanent marker.

2. Peg the clothes onto the washing line with the pegs in no particular order.

3. The children have to re-arrange the pegs to make CVC words.

4. Once a word has been made the pegs can be used again.

5. The child who can make the most words in the time given is the winner.

Phonic family fortunes!

What you need:

- Sheets of A3 paper
- Marker
- Card
- Sticky tack
- Timer
- Buzzer
- Bell

What to do:

1. Prepare short lists of words that start with the letter sounds that you are going to be focussing on.

2. Cover each of the words on your list with a piece of card.

3. Create a crib sheet for your reference during the game.

4. Split the children into two teams.

5. Tell all the children the sound that you are focussing on for this game.

6. Ask them to generate as many words as they can that start with that sound.

7. Set the timer.

8. Once the time is up, each team takes it in turns t call out one of their words.

9. If it is on your list you 'reveal' it and ding your bel

10. If it is not on your list, you sound your buzzer.

11. Three buzzes and you are out!

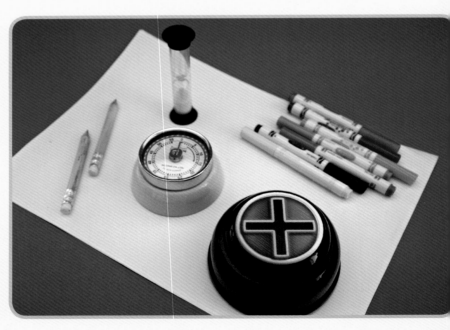

king it forward

Use rhyming words or CVC
words for a greater challenge.

hat's in it for the children?

he children have the opportunity
share their knowledge of initial
und recognition and apply it in
ntext.

fantastic ideas for teaching phonics

Balloon bat

What you need:

- A number of different coloured balloons
- Permanent marker

What to do:

1. Blow up the balloons.
2. Put a different sound onto each one.
3. Ask the children to stand in a circle.
4. Throw in the first balloon. The children have to keep it up in the air by hitting it.
5. Every time they hit it they should say a word that starts with that sound.
6. If a balloon hits the floor it is removed.
7. Keep adding balloons!

Taking it forward

- Change the criteria to rhyming words.

What's in it for the children?

The children are using their phonic knowledge to recognise initial sounds and then apply them in context.

 Health & Safety

Always take care when using balloons, if they get popped pick up the pieces quickly before children put any in their mouths.